Chapter 1: The Call to Action

The morning sun cast a golden hue over the military base as Sergeant First Class JT Williamton stood tall amidst the formation of his fellow soldiers. The air crackled with the energy of anticipation, the sounds of boots shuffling against the pavement and the commands of officers echoing through the crisp morning air. Yet amid the familiar routine of military life, JT's attention was drawn to a murmured conversation drifting through the ranks.

"Financial freedom," the words reached JT's ears, spoken in hushed tones by a soldier nearby.

Intrigued, JT leaned in, his curiosity piqued by the unexpected topic of conversation amidst the disciplined setting of the formation.

"Rat race," another soldier responded, his voice carrying a note of skepticism.

JT furrowed his brow, the term sparking a distant memory buried beneath the responsibilities of his military duties. He recalled hearing similar phrases whispered in the barracks late at night, words tinged with longing and frustration. But now, amidst the structured confines of the formation, the notion of financial freedom seemed to take on a new significance.

"Rat race?" JT echoed, turning to the soldier beside him, a young private with a determined glint in his eye.

The private nodded eagerly, his voice gaining confidence as he spoke. "Yes, SFC. It's like being trapped in a cycle of making money just to make more money, constantly striving but never truly feeling free. But some folks are talking about breaking free from it, finding a way to exit the race altogether."

JT's gaze lingered on the young soldier, his mind racing with thoughts and questions. For years, he had dedicated himself to the service of his country, rising through the ranks with a steadfast determination to lead and protect. But beneath the surface of duty and honor, there had always been a flicker of something more—a desire for something beyond the confines of military life, a yearning for a life of freedom and autonomy.

"Alright, warrior," JT said with a nod, his voice tinged with a hint of intrigue. "Let me know how that works out."

As the formation dispersed and the day's duties commenced, JT found himself unable to shake off the conversation. The idea of financial freedom lingered in his mind, stirring a sense of possibility and curiosity within him. He had always prided himself on his discipline and dedication, but now, amidst the whispers of a life beyond the "rat race," he couldn't help but wonder if there was more to be achieved, more to be gained.

Later that evening, after the last duties of the day had been fulfilled, JT retreated to his quarters, his mind buzzing with thoughts and questions. With a sense of determination burning within him, he fired up his laptop and began to delve into the world of personal finance, scouring articles and forums for information on investing, saving, and building wealth.

As the night wore on, JT found himself drawn deeper into the labyrinth of financial literacy, each new piece of information igniting a spark of possibility within him. Could it be possible, he wondered, to break free from the confines of the "rat race" and chart a course towards true financial independence? And if so, what would it take to achieve such a feat?

With a sense of excitement and anticipation coursing through his veins, JT Williamton embarked on a journey of discovery and empowerment, eager to explore the possibilities that lay ahead on the path to financial freedom.

Chapter 2: The Seed of Curiosity

Days turned into weeks, and JT Williamton's fascination with the concept of financial freedom only deepened. Each evening, after fulfilling his military duties, he found himself drawn back to his quarters, eager to continue his exploration of the world of personal finance.

With a soldier's discipline, JT approached his newfound passion with relentless determination. He devoured books and articles on investing, retirement planning, and wealth management, absorbing every piece of information with an insatiable thirst for knowledge. As he immersed himself in the intricacies of financial literacy, he began to see the world through a new lens, recognizing opportunities and potential where once there had been only uncertainty.

One evening, as JT sat poring over an article about the power of passive income, a spark of inspiration ignited within him. The concept of generating income without active effort resonated deeply with him, offering a glimpse of a future where financial freedom was not just a distant dream, but a tangible reality.

Determined to learn more, JT delved deeper into the world of passive income, exploring strategies such as dividend investing, rental properties, and online businesses. With each new idea he encountered, he felt a sense of excitement and possibility building within him, fueling his desire to break free from the constraints of the "rat race" once and for all.

But JT didn't stop there. Recognizing the importance of diversification in building wealth, he began to explore different asset classes and investment vehicles, from stocks and bonds to real estate and commodities. With each new avenue he explored, he gained a deeper understanding of the intricacies of the financial markets, honing his skills as an investor and strategist.

As JT's knowledge and confidence grew, so too did his determination to share his newfound expertise with his fellow soldiers. He began to host impromptu workshops and informal discussions about personal finance, eager to empower his comrades with the tools and knowledge they needed to take control of their financial futures.

With each workshop he conducted, JT witnessed the spark of possibility ignite in the eyes of his fellow soldiers. He saw the same sense of curiosity and determination that had driven him to explore the world of personal finance reflected in their faces, and it filled him with a sense of pride and purpose.

But amidst the excitement of his own journey and the joy of empowering others, JT remained mindful of the challenges that lay ahead. He knew that achieving financial freedom would require discipline, patience, and a willingness to take calculated risks. Yet with each passing day, he felt more confident in his ability to navigate the complexities of the financial world and chart a course towards a future of freedom and abundance.

As the days turned into months, JT Williamton's journey towards financial freedom gained momentum, fueled by a sense of curiosity, determination, and the unwavering belief that anything was possible with the right knowledge and mindset. And with each step he took along the path to financial independence, he knew that he was one step closer to achieving his dreams.

Chapter 3: The First Steps Towards Financial Independence

As the days stretched into weeks and the weeks into months, JT Williamton's journey towards financial independence gained momentum. Armed with a newfound sense of purpose and a wealth of knowledge acquired through tireless research and exploration, he was ready to take the first steps towards his goal.

The first step JT took was to assess his current financial situation with a critical eye. He meticulously scrutinized his income, expenses, and savings, identifying areas where he could cut costs and optimize his budget. With the precision of a seasoned strategist, he crafted a plan to increase his savings rate and funnel more money towards his investment goals.

With his budget in hand, JT turned his attention to his investment strategy. Drawing upon the principles of diversification and risk management, he carefully constructed a portfolio tailored to his financial goals and risk tolerance. He allocated funds to a mix of asset classes, including stocks, bonds, real estate investment trusts (REITs), and index funds, with the aim of maximizing returns while minimizing risk.

But JT's journey towards financial independence wasn't just about building wealth; it was also about generating multiple streams of income. Inspired by the concept of passive income, he began to explore opportunities to create additional revenue streams outside of his military salary.

One avenue JT pursued was real estate investing. Recognizing the potential for long-term growth and cash flow, he embarked on a search for investment properties in promising markets. With careful research and due diligence, he identified a duplex in a desirable neighborhood and secured financing to purchase the property. He renovated the units and found tenants, turning the property into a source of steady rental income.

In addition to real estate, JT also explored opportunities in the world of entrepreneurship. Drawing upon his skills and experiences, he launched a side business selling handmade crafts online. With dedication and perseverance, he grew the business into a profitable venture, generating supplemental income that bolstered his financial security and accelerated his path towards financial independence.

But perhaps the most impactful aspect of JT's journey was his commitment to mentorship and education. Recognizing the power of knowledge and the importance of empowering others, he dedicated himself to sharing his experiences and insights with his fellow soldiers.

He hosted workshops and seminars on personal finance, covering topics such as budgeting, investing, and retirement planning. He provided one-on-one guidance and support to those who sought his advice, helping them develop personalized financial plans and set achievable goals. And he led by example, demonstrating through his own actions the principles of discipline, perseverance, and strategic thinking required to achieve financial success.

As JT's influence within the military community grew, so too did the culture of financial literacy and empowerment. Soldiers who had once felt overwhelmed and uncertain about their financial futures now found themselves inspired and motivated to take control of their destinies. They began to implement JT's strategies and teachings in their own lives, setting themselves on a path towards financial independence and security.

But amidst the successes and triumphs, JT remained grounded in the knowledge that the journey towards financial independence was not without its challenges. He knew that setbacks and obstacles were inevitable, but he was determined to face them head-on with resilience and determination.

And so, as JT Williamton continued on his journey towards financial independence, he did so with a sense of purpose and optimism, knowing that with each step he took, he was one step closer to achieving his dreams and empowering others to do the same.

Chapter 4: Overcoming Obstacles and Embracing Growth

As JT Williamton's journey towards financial independence continued, he encountered obstacles and challenges that tested his resolve and pushed him to grow in ways he never imagined.

One of the first obstacles JT faced was the volatility of the financial markets. Despite his meticulous research and careful planning, he found himself confronting market downturns and unexpected fluctuations that threatened to derail his investment strategy. But instead of succumbing to panic or despair, JT remained steadfast in his commitment to his long-term goals.

Drawing upon the principles of patience and discipline, JT weathered the storms of uncertainty with a calm and composed demeanor. He resisted the urge to make impulsive decisions based on short-term fluctuations, instead focusing on the fundamentals of his investments and maintaining a long-term perspective. And as the markets eventually rebounded, JT emerged stronger and more resilient than ever, reaffirming his belief in the power of strategic planning and steadfast resolve.

Another obstacle JT encountered on his journey was the temptation of instant gratification. As his side business and investment portfolio began to generate returns, he found himself faced with the temptation to indulge in lavish purchases and extravagant luxuries. But JT recognized that succumbing to these temptations would only hinder his progress towards financial independence.

With discipline and restraint, JT resisted the lure of instant gratification and instead focused on reinvesting his profits back into his business and investment portfolio. He remained mindful of his long-term goals and the sacrifices he was willing to make in order to achieve them, knowing that the path to financial independence required discipline, patience, and a willingness to delay gratification in the pursuit of a greater purpose.

But perhaps the greatest obstacle JT faced on his journey was the fear of failure. As he ventured into unfamiliar territory and pursued ambitious goals, he was plagued by doubts and insecurities about his ability to succeed. But instead of allowing fear to paralyze him, JT embraced it as a natural part of the growth process.

With courage and determination, JT confronted his fears head-on, recognizing that failure was not an end but rather a stepping stone on the path to success. He embraced a growth mindset, viewing challenges as opportunities for learning and growth, and refusing to let setbacks define him or his journey.

Through perseverance and resilience, JT emerged from each challenge stronger and more determined than before. He learned valuable lessons about resilience, adaptability, and the importance of staying true to oneself in the face of adversity. And with each obstacle overcome, he grew more confident in his ability to navigate the twists and turns of his journey towards financial independence.

But amidst the trials and tribulations, JT also experienced moments of profound growth and transformation. He discovered new strengths and talents within himself, honed his skills as a leader and mentor, and forged deep and meaningful connections with his fellow soldiers and peers.

As JT reflected on the obstacles he had overcome and the growth he had experienced, he realized that his journey towards financial independence was not just about building wealth, but about becoming the best version of himself and inspiring others to do the same. And with renewed determination and optimism, he set his sights on the horizon, ready to face whatever challenges and opportunities lay ahead on the path to financial freedom.

Chapter 5: The Journey Deepens: Navigating Peaks and Valleys

As JT Williamton's journey towards financial independence progressed, he found himself navigating a landscape of peaks and valleys, each one presenting its own unique set of challenges and opportunities.

One of the peaks JT encountered on his journey was the realization of the power of compounding returns. As he diligently contributed to his investment portfolio and reinvested his dividends and interest, he began to witness the remarkable effects of compounding over time. With each passing year, his wealth grew exponentially, accelerating his progress towards his financial goals.

JT's commitment to discipline and consistency also bore fruit in other areas of his life. He found himself achieving greater balance and harmony between his military duties, his side business, and his personal pursuits. With careful planning and time management, he was able to allocate his resources effectively, maximizing his productivity and efficiency in pursuit of his goals.

But amidst the peaks of success, JT also encountered valleys of uncertainty and doubt. He faced setbacks and challenges that tested his resolve and forced him to confront his deepest fears and insecurities. Whether it was a failed investment, a setback in his side business, or a personal hardship, JT learned to embrace adversity as a natural part of the journey towards financial independence.

In the face of these challenges, JT drew upon the lessons he had learned along the way—lessons of resilience, adaptability, and the importance of staying true to oneself in the face of adversity. He refused to be defined by his setbacks, choosing instead to view them as opportunities for growth and learning.

One of the most significant valleys JT encountered on his journey was the global financial crisis. As the economy faltered and markets tumbled, JT found himself grappling with uncertainty and anxiety about the future. But instead of succumbing to fear, he remained steadfast in his commitment to his long-term goals, trusting in the resilience of the markets and his own ability to weather the storm.

JT's journey through the valley of the financial crisis taught him valuable lessons about the importance of diversification, risk management, and maintaining a long-term perspective. He emerged from the crisis stronger and more resilient than ever, reaffirming his belief in the power of strategic planning and disciplined execution in achieving financial success.

But perhaps the most profound lesson JT learned from his journey through the peaks and valleys was the importance of staying true to his values and priorities. As he navigated the twists and turns of his journey towards financial independence, he remained grounded in his commitment to integrity, honesty, and the well-being of those around him.

As JT reflected on the peaks and valleys of his journey, he realized that each experience had shaped him in profound ways, molding him into the person he was meant to become. And with renewed determination and optimism, he set his sights on the horizon, ready to face whatever challenges and opportunities lay ahead on the path to financial freedom.

Chapter 6: Reflections of the Past, Visions of the Future

As JT Williamton's journey towards financial independence continued, he found himself reflecting on the past with a sense of nostalgia and gratitude. Memories from his childhood flooded back to him, reminding him of the journey that had brought him to where he stood today.

In a quiet moment of reflection, JT found himself transported back to his childhood home—a small house nestled in a tight-knit community where neighbors knew each other by name and everyone looked out for one another. He recalled the simple pleasures of his youth—the sound of laughter echoing through the streets, the warmth of family gatherings, and the sense of security that came from knowing he was loved and supported.

But amidst the fond memories, JT also recalled the challenges and hardships he had faced growing up. Raised by a single mother who worked tirelessly to make ends meet, JT learned the value of hard work and perseverance from an early age. He remembered the sacrifices his mother had made to provide for him and his siblings, and the lessons of resilience and determination she had instilled in him through her own example.

In one vivid flashback, JT recalled a pivotal moment from his childhood—a day when his mother sat him down and imparted a piece of wisdom that would stay with him for the rest of his life.

"Life is full of ups and downs, son," she had said, her voice tinged with a mixture of strength and vulnerability. "But no matter what challenges you may face, remember that you have the power to overcome them. You are stronger than you know, and with determination and courage, you can achieve anything you set your mind to."

JT carried his mother's words with him like a guiding light, drawing strength from them in moments of uncertainty and doubt. And as he navigated the peaks and valleys of his journey towards financial independence, he found himself returning to her wisdom time and time again, finding solace and inspiration in her unwavering belief in his ability to succeed.

With a renewed sense of purpose and determination, JT turned his gaze towards the future, envisioning the life of abundance and fulfillment he dreamed of creating for himself and his loved ones. He saw himself achieving his financial goals, building wealth and security for the future, and living a life of freedom and autonomy that surpassed even his wildest dreams.

But amidst the visions of the future, JT also recognized the importance of staying grounded in the present moment. He knew that the journey towards financial independence was not just about reaching a destination, but about savoring the journey itself—the lessons learned, the relationships forged, and the memories made along the way.

With a sense of gratitude for the past, a vision for the future, and a commitment to living fully in the present, JT Williamton embarked on the next phase of his journey towards financial independence, ready to embrace whatever challenges and opportunities lay ahead with courage, determination, and an unwavering belief in the power of possibility.

Chapter 7: Shadows of the Past: A Soldier's Dilemma

As JT Williamton's journey towards financial independence unfolded, he found himself grappling with memories of a different kind—a time when he was faced with the weight of life-and-death decisions in the heart of a warzone.

It was a sweltering day in Iraq, the sun beating down relentlessly as JT and his fellow soldiers prepared for a critical three-month operation in the heart of enemy territory. The mission was fraught with danger and uncertainty, and JT knew that the success of the operation hinged on his ability to make split-second decisions under pressure.

In a vivid flashback, JT found himself transported back to that fateful day, the memories as vivid as if they had happened only moments ago. He remembered the tension in the air as the convoy rumbled through the dusty streets, every sense heightened in anticipation of the dangers that lay ahead.

As they approached their destination, JT's unit came under heavy fire from enemy insurgents, their bullets whizzing past with deadly accuracy. In the chaos and confusion of the firefight, JT found himself faced with a series of impossible choices—choices that would determine the fate of his fellow soldiers and the success of the mission.

With bullets flying and explosions ringing in his ears, JT had to think fast, drawing upon his training and instincts to guide his unit to safety. He issued orders with precision and clarity, directing his soldiers with calm and authority in the midst of chaos. And as the firefight raged on, JT made split-second decisions that would ultimately determine the outcome of the operation.

In one harrowing moment, JT found himself confronted with a dilemma that tested his principles and his resolve. With enemy forces closing in and casualties mounting, he had to make a choice—risk the safety of his unit to rescue a wounded comrade, or leave them behind to ensure the success of the mission.

In the end, JT chose to prioritize the safety of his unit above all else, knowing that the success of the mission depended on their ability to work together as a cohesive unit. It was a decision that weighed heavily on his conscience, but one that he knew was necessary to ensure that everyone made it home alive.

As JT reflected on the events of that day, he felt a mixture of pride and sorrow wash over him. Pride in the bravery and resilience of his fellow soldiers, who had faced danger with unwavering courage. Sorrow for the sacrifices that had been made, and the lives that had been lost in service to their country.

But amidst the memories of war and sacrifice, JT also felt a sense of gratitude—for the bonds of brotherhood forged in the heat of battle, for the lessons learned in the crucible of conflict, and for the opportunity to serve something greater than himself.

With a renewed sense of purpose and determination, JT carried the memories of his time in Iraq with him as he continued on his journey towards financial independence. He knew that the lessons learned on the battlefield would serve him well in the challenges that lay ahead, and that the courage and resilience he had demonstrated in the face of adversity would guide him through whatever obstacles he encountered along the way.

Chapter 8: Lost in the Fog: Rediscovering Purpose Amidst Adversity

In the aftermath of a particularly intense combat mission, JT Williamton found himself grappling with a profound sense of disorientation. The chaos and violence of the battlefield had left him shaken, his mind clouded with a dense fog that obscured his memories and dulled his senses.

As he emerged from the haze of combat, JT found himself grappling with a disturbing realization—he had forgotten everything he had learned on his journey towards financial independence. The principles of discipline, patience, and strategic planning that had guided him through the peaks and valleys of his journey were now distant echoes in his mind, drowned out by the clamor of war.

In a moment of clarity amidst the confusion, JT recognized the gravity of the situation. Without the knowledge and skills he had acquired on his journey, he was adrift in a sea of uncertainty, unsure of how to navigate the challenges that lay ahead. But instead of succumbing to despair, JT resolved to face the adversity head-on, determined to rediscover his purpose and reclaim the lessons he had learned.

With a sense of determination and resilience, JT set out on a journey of rediscovery, seeking to reconnect with the wisdom and insights that had guided him in the past. He immersed himself in books and articles on personal finance, devouring every piece of information with a hunger born of necessity. He attended workshops and seminars, eager to glean new insights and perspectives from experts in the field. And he sought out mentors and advisors, drawing upon their wisdom and guidance to help him navigate the challenges of rebuilding his financial knowledge from the ground up.

But as JT delved deeper into his quest for knowledge, he encountered unexpected obstacles and setbacks along the way. The memories of war and trauma lingered like ghosts in his mind, haunting him with their echoes of pain and suffering. The demands of military duty threatened to consume his time and energy, leaving little room for the pursuit of personal growth and development. And the fear of failure loomed large, casting a shadow of doubt over his ability to reclaim the success he had once achieved.

Yet amidst the adversity, JT refused to be deterred. With each setback he encountered, he found renewed determination and resolve, drawing upon the strength and resilience he had honed on the battlefield. He embraced the challenges as opportunities for growth and learning, knowing that the journey towards financial independence was not just about reaching a destination, but about the process of becoming the best version of himself.

And as JT navigated the twists and turns of his journey, he began to feel the fog of confusion slowly lifting, replaced by a newfound clarity and purpose. With each step he took, he felt himself drawing closer to rediscovering the knowledge and insights that had once guided him towards financial independence. And with each challenge he overcame, he grew stronger and more resilient, ready to face whatever obstacles lay ahead on the path to reclaiming his success.

Chapter 9: A Journey of Remembrance

Determined to reclaim the knowledge and insights he had lost amidst the chaos of combat, JT Williamton embarked on a side adventure—an expedition into the wilderness that would challenge him both physically and mentally, and ultimately lead him to rediscover the wisdom he sought.

With a map in hand and a sense of purpose in his heart, JT set out into the rugged wilderness, guided by the whispers of a distant memory that beckoned him towards a hidden treasure—a treasure of knowledge and understanding that held the key to unlocking the secrets of his past.

As he journeyed deeper into the wilderness, JT found himself confronting the untamed beauty of nature in all its glory—the towering mountains, the rushing rivers, and the whispering forests that seemed to pulse with life and energy. Each step he took brought him closer to his destination, yet also deeper into the labyrinth of his own thoughts and memories.

Along the way, JT encountered challenges and obstacles that tested his resolve and pushed him to his limits. He traversed treacherous terrain, battled fierce storms, and faced encounters with wild animals that stirred primal instincts within him. Yet through it all, he remained steadfast in his determination to uncover the truth that lay hidden within the depths of his own mind.

As JT journeyed deeper into the wilderness, he found himself drawn towards a towering peak that loomed on the horizon—a peak shrouded in mystery and legend, said to hold the key to unlocking the secrets of the past. With each step he took towards the summit, he felt a sense of anticipation building within him, knowing that he was on the brink of a discovery that would change him forever.

Finally, after days of arduous trekking, JT reached the summit of the mountain, his breath catching in his throat as he beheld the breathtaking vista that unfolded before him. And there, amidst the sweeping panorama of snow-capped peaks and rolling valleys, he found what he had been searching for all along—a moment of clarity and revelation that washed over him like a wave.

In that moment of profound realization, JT remembered everything—the lessons he had learned, the wisdom he had gained, and the journey that had brought him to where he stood today. He saw with crystal clarity the path that lay before him, illuminated by the light of understanding and insight.

With a sense of peace and purpose washing over him, JT descended from the summit, his heart light and his mind clear. And as he journeyed back to civilization, he carried with him the knowledge and wisdom he had rediscovered—the knowledge that would guide him on the path to reclaiming his success and achieving his dreams once more.

Chapter 10: Reclaiming Success

With the clarity and wisdom he had rediscovered during his journey of remembrance, JT Williamton returned to his quest for financial independence with renewed vigor and determination. Armed with the knowledge and insights he had reclaimed, he set out to retrace his steps and rebuild the foundation of success he had once achieved.

As he immersed himself once more in the world of personal finance, JT found himself reconnecting with the principles and strategies that had guided him on his journey before. He revisited the lessons he had learned about budgeting, investing, and building wealth, recommitting himself to the disciplined approach that had served him well in the past.

With each passing day, JT felt himself regaining momentum and clarity, his confidence growing with each step he took towards his financial goals. He made a plan to increase his savings rate, setting aside a portion of his income each month to invest in a diversified portfolio of assets. He revisited his investment strategy, carefully rebalancing his portfolio to align with his long-term objectives and risk tolerance.

But JT's journey towards financial independence was not just about reclaiming his success—it was also about growth and evolution. With the wisdom he had gained from his experiences, he began to explore new avenues and opportunities for building wealth, expanding his horizons beyond the familiar confines of his previous endeavors.

One area JT focused on was entrepreneurship. Inspired by the success of his side business before, he set out to explore new ventures and opportunities for generating additional streams of income. Drawing upon his skills and experiences, he launched a new business venture, leveraging his knowledge and expertise to create value and generate profits in the marketplace.

In addition to entrepreneurship, JT also explored the world of passive income, seeking out opportunities to create sustainable sources of revenue that would continue to grow and expand over time. He invested in rental properties, dividend-paying stocks, and other income-generating assets, diversifying his portfolio and maximizing his potential for long-term wealth accumulation.

As JT continued on his journey towards financial independence, he found himself inspired by the progress he was making and the possibilities that lay ahead. He remained committed to his goals, knowing that the journey would not always be easy, but confident in his ability to overcome any obstacles that stood in his way.

And with each step he took towards reclaiming his success, JT felt a sense of pride and satisfaction wash over him—a reminder of the resilience and determination that had brought him to where he stood today, and the limitless potential that lay within him to achieve his dreams.

Chapter 11: The Power of Mentorship

As JT Williamton continued his journey towards financial independence, he recognized the invaluable role that mentorship played in his growth and development. Drawing upon the wisdom and guidance of those who had walked the path before him, JT sought out mentors and advisors who could offer insights and perspectives to help him navigate the challenges and opportunities that lay ahead.

One of JT's most influential mentors was a retired military veteran who had achieved financial independence after years of dedicated service. Through their conversations and interactions, JT gained invaluable insights into the principles and strategies that had guided his mentor to success.

The retired veteran shared stories of his own journey towards financial independence, offering lessons learned from both his successes and failures along the way. He emphasized the importance of discipline, patience, and perseverance in achieving long-term financial goals, and encouraged JT to stay focused on the bigger picture, even in the face of adversity.

With his mentor's guidance, JT refined his investment strategy, fine-tuning his approach to align with his long-term objectives and risk tolerance. He gained confidence in his ability to navigate the complexities of the financial markets, knowing that he had a seasoned mentor by his side to offer guidance and support along the way.

But mentorship was not just about receiving advice—it was also about giving back and paying it forward. Inspired by the support he had received from his own mentors, JT sought out opportunities to mentor and empower others on their own journeys towards financial independence.

He hosted workshops and seminars, sharing his experiences and insights with fellow soldiers and peers who were eager to learn and grow. He provided one-on-one guidance and support, helping individuals develop personalized financial plans and overcome obstacles standing in their way.

Through his mentorship efforts, JT witnessed the transformative power of knowledge and guidance in the lives of those he touched. He saw fellow soldiers and peers gain confidence and clarity as they navigated their own financial journeys, inspired by JT's example and empowered to take control of their destinies.

And as JT continued to mentor and empower others, he found that he gained as much from the experience as those he helped. He deepened his own understanding of financial principles and strategies, honed his skills as a leader and communicator, and forged deep and meaningful connections with those he mentored.

With each interaction, JT was reminded of the profound impact that mentorship could have on the lives of others, and the importance of giving back and supporting those who followed in his footsteps. And as he continued on his journey towards financial independence, he knew that he would always carry with him the lessons and insights he had gained from his mentors, guiding him towards success and fulfillment in all areas of life.

Chapter 12: Embracing the Journey

As JT Williamton delved deeper into his journey towards financial independence, he came to realize that success was not just about reaching a destination—it was about embracing the journey itself. With each passing day, he found himself growing more attuned to the rhythms of life, savoring the moments of joy, learning, and growth that filled his days.

One of the most profound realizations JT had along his journey was the importance of mindset in achieving success. He recognized that mindset played a crucial role in shaping his attitudes and behaviors towards money, and that cultivating a positive and abundance mindset was key to unlocking his full potential.

With this newfound awareness, JT began to practice gratitude and mindfulness in his daily life, focusing on the blessings and opportunities that surrounded him rather than dwelling on scarcity or lack. He celebrated his successes, no matter how small, and embraced setbacks as opportunities for growth and learning.

In addition to mindset, JT also came to appreciate the importance of balance and harmony in his pursuit of financial independence. He recognized that true wealth encompassed more than just monetary riches—it encompassed health, relationships, personal fulfillment, and a sense of purpose and meaning in life.

With this in mind, JT took steps to nurture all areas of his life, prioritizing self-care, spending quality time with loved ones, and pursuing passions and interests outside of his financial goals. He found fulfillment in giving back to his community, volunteering his time and resources to causes he was passionate about, and making a positive impact in the lives of others.

As JT continued to grow and evolve on his journey, he found himself surrounded by a community of like-minded individuals who shared his vision for financial independence and personal fulfillment. He formed deep and meaningful connections with fellow soldiers, peers, and mentors who inspired and supported him along the way, and who celebrated his successes as their own.

And as JT reflected on the journey he had undertaken and the lessons he had learned along the way, he knew that he was exactly where he was meant to be—in the midst of a journey filled with challenges and triumphs, setbacks and victories, but above all, with endless opportunities for growth, fulfillment, and joy.

With a sense of gratitude and purpose filling his heart, JT Williamton embraced the journey towards financial independence with open arms, knowing that the path ahead was filled with infinite possibilities, and that the best was yet to come.

Chapter 13: Achieving Financial Independence

As JT Williamton journeyed further along the path towards financial independence, he found himself approaching a significant milestone—the realization of his long-held dream of achieving true financial freedom. With each passing day, he could feel the momentum building, bringing him ever closer to his ultimate goal.

One of the key milestones JT reached on his journey was the achievement of a robust and diversified investment portfolio. Through careful planning and disciplined execution, he had built a portfolio that generated passive income streams from various sources, including stocks, bonds, real estate, and business ventures.

With his investment portfolio steadily growing, JT began to experience the benefits of passive income firsthand. He no longer relied solely on his military salary for financial security, but instead enjoyed the freedom and flexibility that came from having multiple streams of income supporting him.

Another milestone JT achieved was the attainment of financial stability and security for himself and his loved ones. Through prudent budgeting and strategic planning, he had built a solid foundation of savings and emergency funds, providing a safety net in times of uncertainty and allowing him to weather any storms that might arise.

But perhaps the most significant milestone JT reached was the moment when he was able to declare himself financially independent—the moment when he no longer needed to rely on a traditional job for income, but instead had the freedom to pursue his passions and interests on his own terms.

With a sense of pride and accomplishment, JT celebrated this momentous occasion, knowing that it was the culmination of years of hard work, discipline, and sacrifice. He had overcome countless obstacles and challenges along the way, but through sheer determination and perseverance, he had emerged victorious, achieving a level of financial freedom that few ever attain.

As JT basked in the glow of his success, he couldn't help but feel a sense of gratitude for the journey he had undertaken and the lessons he had learned along the way. He knew that the path to financial independence had not always been easy, but it had been worth every moment, for it had led him to this point of fulfillment and joy.

And as he looked towards the future, JT knew that his journey was far from over. With financial independence now within his grasp, he was free to pursue his passions and dreams with renewed vigor and enthusiasm, knowing that the possibilities were endless and that the best was yet to come.

Chapter 14: A New Chapter Begins

With financial independence achieved, JT Williamton found himself standing at the threshold of a new chapter in his life—a chapter filled with endless possibilities and opportunities for growth, fulfillment, and contribution.

One of the first things JT did upon reaching this milestone was to take time to reflect on his journey—the highs and lows, the challenges and triumphs, and the lessons learned along the way. He felt a profound sense of gratitude for the experiences that had shaped him, and for the support and guidance he had received from mentors, peers, and loved ones.

But JT also knew that achieving financial independence was not the end of his journey—it was just the beginning. With newfound freedom and autonomy, he was eager to explore new horizons and pursue his passions and interests with renewed vigor.

One area JT was particularly excited to explore was philanthropy. Inspired by the generosity of those who had supported him on his journey, he felt a deep desire to give back to his community and make a positive impact in the world.

He began by volunteering his time and resources to causes he was passionate about, getting involved in local charities and nonprofit organizations that were making a difference in the lives of others. He also established a charitable foundation, dedicated to supporting initiatives that promoted education, health, and economic empowerment in underserved communities.

In addition to philanthropy, JT also focused on personal growth and development, seeking out opportunities to expand his knowledge and skills in areas outside of finance. He enrolled in courses and workshops on topics ranging from leadership and entrepreneurship to personal wellness and spirituality, eager to continue evolving as a person and a leader.

But amidst all the excitement and possibilities of this new chapter, JT also remained grounded in the values and principles that had guided him on his journey thus far. He continued to live frugally and consciously, mindful of the importance of stewardship and sustainability in all aspects of his life.

And as JT embarked on this new chapter, he did so with a sense of optimism and excitement, knowing that the journey ahead would be filled with challenges and opportunities, setbacks and triumphs, but above all, with the potential for growth, fulfillment, and joy. And with every step he took, he knew that he was living a life of purpose and meaning, making a difference in the world and leaving a legacy that would endure for generations to come.

Chapter 15: Passing on the Torch

As JT Williamton continued to navigate his newfound freedom and purpose, he recognized the importance of passing on the lessons he had learned and the values he held dear to the next generation. He felt a deep sense of responsibility to mentor and empower others, just as he had been mentored and empowered on his own journey towards financial independence.

One of the ways JT sought to pass on the torch was through education. He dedicated himself to teaching financial literacy and empowerment to young soldiers and peers, equipping them with the knowledge and skills they needed to take control of their financial futures and build lives of abundance and fulfillment.

JT also became actively involved in initiatives aimed at supporting military veterans in their transition to civilian life. He volunteered his time and resources to organizations that provided job training, educational opportunities, and mental health support to veterans, ensuring that those who had served their country received the assistance they deserved.

But perhaps the most impactful way JT passed on the torch was through his own example. He lived his life with integrity, generosity, and purpose, serving as a role model for others to emulate. He demonstrated the power of discipline, perseverance, and resilience in the face of adversity, inspiring those around him to strive for greatness in their own lives.

And as JT continued to pass on the torch to the next generation, he knew that he was leaving a legacy that would endure long after he was gone. He had not only achieved financial independence for himself, but had empowered countless others to do the same, creating a ripple effect of positive change that would continue to reverberate through the years.

With a sense of fulfillment and pride, JT Williamton looked towards the future, knowing that he had made a difference in the world and left a lasting impact on those he had touched. And as he passed on the torch to the next generation, he did so with the knowledge that the journey towards financial independence was not just about individual success, but about lifting others up and creating a better world for all.

Chapter 16: A Legacy of Impact

As JT Williamton reflected on his journey, he realized that his legacy extended far beyond his own achievements—it was a legacy of impact, shaped by the lives he had touched and the difference he had made in the world.

One of the most profound aspects of JT's legacy was the ripple effect of positive change he had created through his mentorship and empowerment efforts. The soldiers and peers he had mentored and inspired went on to achieve their own financial independence, passing on the knowledge and wisdom they had gained to others in turn.

Through his philanthropic endeavors, JT had also left a tangible mark on the world, supporting initiatives that made a real difference in the lives of those in need. Whether it was providing access to education for underserved communities, supporting veterans in their transition to civilian life, or addressing pressing social and environmental issues, JT's charitable contributions had a lasting impact that extended far beyond his own lifetime.

But perhaps the most enduring aspect of JT's legacy was the values and principles he had instilled in others—the importance of integrity, perseverance, and compassion in all aspects of life. By living his life with authenticity and purpose, JT had set an example for others to follow, inspiring them to strive for greatness and make a positive difference in the world.

As JT looked towards the future, he knew that his legacy would continue to grow and evolve, carried forward by those he had touched along the way. He felt a deep sense of gratitude for the opportunities he had been given and the people who had supported him on his journey, knowing that his life had been enriched immeasurably by their presence.

And as he embraced the next chapter of his life with open arms, JT Williamton did so with a sense of peace and fulfillment, knowing that he had lived a life of purpose and meaning, and that his legacy would endure for generations to come.

Chapter 17: Beyond Boundaries

As JT Williamton's story unfolded, it transcended the boundaries of his own life, reaching across time and space to inspire others in ways he could never have imagined. His journey towards financial independence had become a beacon of hope and possibility, illuminating the path for countless individuals who dared to dream of a better future.

JT's story spread far and wide, resonating with people from all walks of life who found inspiration in his resilience, determination, and unwavering commitment to his goals. From soldiers on the front lines to civilians in far-off lands, JT's message of empowerment and possibility touched hearts and minds around the world.

Through the power of technology and communication, JT's story reached even the most remote corners of the globe, sparking conversations and igniting passions in places he had never been. His journey became a source of motivation and encouragement for those facing their own struggles and challenges, reminding them that anything was possible with dedication and perseverance.

But perhaps the most profound impact of JT's story was the sense of community and connection it fostered among those who shared in his journey. People came together, united by a common purpose and a shared commitment to personal growth and empowerment, forming bonds that transcended borders and boundaries.

As JT witnessed the ripple effect of his story spreading across the world, he felt a profound sense of gratitude and humility. He knew that his journey had become so much more than just his own—it had become a collective journey, shared by countless individuals who had been touched and inspired by his example.

And as he looked towards the future, JT knew that the impact of his story would continue to grow and evolve, touching the lives of countless others in ways he could never have imagined. He felt a deep sense of pride in knowing that his journey had made a difference in the world, and that his legacy would endure for generations to come.

With a heart full of gratitude and a spirit filled with hope, JT Williamton embraced the boundless possibilities of the future, knowing that his story would continue to inspire and empower others to reach for the stars and achieve their dreams, no matter where they may be.

Chapter 18: The Endless Journey

As JT Williamton's story came to a close, it became clear that his journey towards financial independence was not just a destination, but an endless journey—a journey of growth, discovery, and transformation that would continue to unfold for the rest of his days.

With each passing day, JT found new opportunities for learning and growth, new challenges to overcome, and new dreams to pursue. He embraced the journey with open arms, knowing that it was the journey itself that held the true value and meaning in life.

Along the way, JT continued to live his life with purpose and passion, making a positive impact in the world and leaving a legacy that would endure for generations to come. He remained committed to his values and principles, guided by the wisdom he had gained on his journey and the lessons he had learned along the way.

And as JT looked back on his journey—the highs and lows, the victories and defeats—he knew that he wouldn't change a single moment of it. For it was through the challenges and struggles that he had grown the most, and it was through the triumphs and successes that he had found the most joy and fulfillment.

With a heart full of gratitude and a soul filled with peace, JT Williamton embraced the endless journey before him, knowing that with each step he took, he was moving closer to his true purpose and destiny. And as he set out on the path ahead, he did so with a sense of excitement and anticipation, eager to see where the journey would take him next.

Chapter 19: The Legacy Lives On

As JT Williamton's journey continued, his legacy lived on in the hearts and minds of those he had touched along the way. His story had become a source of inspiration and empowerment for countless individuals, igniting a spark of hope and possibility in the darkest corners of the world.

Through the power of his example and the impact of his actions, JT had created a ripple effect of positive change that extended far beyond his own lifetime. His legacy lived on in the lives he had transformed, the dreams he had inspired, and the communities he had uplifted.

But JT's legacy was not just about the lives he had touched—it was also about the values and principles he had embodied throughout his journey. His commitment to integrity, perseverance, and compassion had set a standard for others to follow, guiding them on their own paths towards greatness.

As time passed and the world changed, JT's legacy continued to evolve, adapting to the needs and challenges of each new generation. His story remained a timeless reminder of the power of resilience, determination, and belief in oneself to overcome even the greatest of obstacles.

And as the years went by, JT's name became synonymous with hope, possibility, and the endless potential of the human spirit. His story was told and retold, passed down from one generation to the next as a testament to the enduring power of the human spirit to overcome adversity and achieve greatness.

In the end, JT Williamton's legacy was not measured by the wealth he had amassed or the accolades he had received, but by the lives he had touched and the hearts he had inspired. His journey had left an indelible mark on the world, reminding us all that with courage, determination, and a willingness to embrace the journey, anything is possible. And as long as his story lived on, so too would the legacy of JT Williamton, the warrior of wealth.

Chapter 20: The Final Chapter

As JT Williamton's journey drew to a close, he found himself reflecting on the incredible odyssey that had brought him to this moment. It had been a journey filled with highs and lows, triumphs and challenges, but through it all, he had remained steadfast in his pursuit of financial independence and personal fulfillment.

With each passing day, JT had discovered new depths of resilience and determination within himself, pushing past obstacles and setbacks to reach new heights of success. He had embraced the lessons learned along the way, growing wiser and stronger with each experience, and forging a path that was uniquely his own.

But as JT looked back on his journey, he knew that the true measure of his success lay not in the wealth he had accumulated or the achievements he had attained, but in the impact he had made on the lives of others. He had empowered countless individuals to take control of their financial futures, inspiring them to dream big and reach for the stars.

And as JT's journey came to an end, he found himself filled with a profound sense of gratitude—for the experiences he had shared, the lessons he had learned, and the people who had supported him along the way. He knew that he was blessed beyond measure, and that his life had been enriched immeasurably by the journey he had undertaken.

With a heart full of gratitude and a soul at peace, JT Williamton bid farewell to his journey, knowing that his legacy would live on in the hearts and minds of those he had touched. And as he stepped into the next chapter of his life, he did so with a sense of excitement and anticipation, eager to see what new adventures awaited him on the horizon.

And so, as the final chapter of JT Williamton's story came to a close, one thing was certain—the warrior of wealth had left an indelible mark on the world, and his legacy would endure for generations to come.

Epilogue: A Lasting Legacy

In the years that followed, JT Williamton's story continued to inspire and uplift those who heard it. His journey towards financial independence had become a timeless tale of perseverance, resilience, and the power of the human spirit to overcome adversity and achieve greatness.

As his story spread far and wide, it reached the ears of countless individuals who found themselves inspired to take control of their own financial futures and pursue their dreams with renewed vigor and determination. From soldiers on the battlefield to civilians in the boardroom, JT's message of empowerment resonated deeply with people from all walks of life.

But perhaps the most profound impact of JT's legacy was the lasting change it brought about in the world. Through his philanthropic efforts and commitment to giving back, JT had left a tangible mark on the lives of countless individuals, empowering them to build better futures for themselves and their communities.

And as time went on, JT's name became synonymous with hope, possibility, and the transformative power of personal growth and empowerment. His story continued to be told and retold, passed down from one generation to the next as a reminder of the limitless potential that lies within each and every one of us.

In the end, JT Williamton's legacy was not measured by the wealth he had amassed or the accolades he had received, but by the lives he had touched and the hearts he had inspired. His journey had left an indelible mark on the world, reminding us all that with courage, determination, and a willingness to embrace the journey, anything is possible.

And so, as the sun set on JT Williamton's remarkable journey, one thing was certain—his legacy would endure for generations to come, a beacon of hope and inspiration for all who dared to dream of a better tomorrow.

As the years passed, JT Williamton's legacy continued to thrive, evolving in ways he could have never imagined. His story became ingrained in the fabric of society, celebrated as a testament to the power of perseverance, resilience, and the unwavering pursuit of one's dreams.

JT's impact extended far beyond the realm of finance, inspiring individuals from all walks of life to embrace their own journeys of self-discovery and personal growth. His message resonated with people of all ages, backgrounds, and circumstances, reminding them that no dream was too big, and no obstacle too insurmountable.

In honor of JT's contributions to the world, a foundation was established in his name, dedicated to supporting initiatives that promoted financial literacy, empowerment, and social justice. Through the foundation's efforts, JT's legacy continued to thrive, leaving an enduring mark on future generations.

But perhaps the most meaningful legacy of all was the impact JT had on those closest to him—the soldiers he mentored, the peers he inspired, and the loved ones who stood by his side through it all. To them, JT was more than just a mentor or a friend—he was a beacon of hope, a guiding light in times of darkness, and a source of unwavering support and encouragement.

As JT's story continued to be told and retold, it served as a reminder that true wealth is not measured in material possessions, but in the lives we touch and the difference we make in the world. And though JT's journey had come to an end, his legacy would live on forever, a testament to the power of the human spirit to overcome adversity and achieve greatness.
In the years following JT Williamton's passing, his legacy remained vibrant and enduring, continuing to inspire generations to come. The foundation established in his honor flourished, expanding its reach and impact across the globe. Through scholarships, educational programs, and community initiatives, the JT Williamton Foundation empowered countless individuals to pursue their dreams and create positive change in their communities.

But JT's legacy extended far beyond the foundation that bore his name. His story continued to resonate with people from all walks of life, serving as a source of motivation and encouragement in times of uncertainty and adversity. From classrooms to boardrooms, his principles of resilience, integrity, and compassion guided individuals in their personal and professional pursuits.

In addition to his philanthropic endeavors, JT's impact endured through the lives he had touched directly. The soldiers he had mentored went on to become leaders in their own right, passing on the lessons they had learned from JT to future generations of servicemen and women. His peers and loved ones carried on his legacy, honoring his memory through acts of kindness, generosity, and service to others.

As time passed, JT Williamton became more than just a man—he became a symbol of hope, possibility, and the transformative power of perseverance. His story continued to inspire countless individuals to reach for their dreams, no matter the obstacles they faced. And though he may have left this world, his spirit lived on in the hearts and minds of all who were touched by his remarkable journey.

And so, as the years turned into decades, JT Williamton's legacy remained an indelible part of the human experience—a reminder of the extraordinary potential that lies within each of us to make a difference in the world and leave a lasting impact on future generations.

www.ingramcontent.com/pod-product-compliance
Lightning Source LLC
Chambersburg PA
CBHW051536240526
45471CB00020B/2993